T0071125

RALPH VAUGHAN WILLIAMS

FOUR LAST SONGS

Four Last Songs

Words by Ursula Vaughan Williams

Arranged for SATB choir and piano by Jonathan Wikeley

OXFORD
UNIVERSITY PRESS

OXFORD
UNIVERSITY PRESS

Great Clarendon Street, Oxford OX2 6DP,
United Kingdom

Oxford University Press is a department of the University of Oxford.
It furthers the University's objective of excellence in research, scholarship,
and education by publishing worldwide. Oxford is a registered trade mark of
Oxford University Press in the UK and in certain other countries

© 1960 Oxford University Press. This arrangement © Oxford University Press 2023.

The right of Ralph Vaughan Williams to be named as the Composer of this Work
has been asserted in accordance with the Copyright, Design and Patents Act 1988
The right of Ursula Vaughan Williams to be named as the Author of this Work
has been asserted in accordance with the Copyright, Design and Patents Act 1988
The right of Jonathan Wikeley to be named as the Arranger of this Work
has been asserted in accordance with the Copyright, Design and Patents Act 1988

First published 2023

Impression: 1

All rights reserved. No part of this publication may be reproduced,
stored in a retrieval system, or transmitted, in any form or by any means,
without the prior permission in writing of Oxford University Press

Permission to perform this work in public (except in the course of
divine worship) should normally be obtained from a local performing right
licensing organization, unless the owner or the occupier of the premises
being used already holds a licence from such an organization.
Likewise, permission to make and exploit a recording of this work
should be obtained from a local mechanical copyright licensing organization

Enquiries concerning reproduction outside the scope of the above
should be directed to the Music Rights Department, Oxford University Press,
at music.permissions.uk@oup.com or at the address above

ISBN 978-0-19-356416-9

Music origination by Ralph Woodward
Printed in Great Britain on acid-free paper by
Halstan & Co. Ltd, Amersham, Bucks.

Contents

1. Procris 4
2. Tired 12
3. Hands, Eyes, and Heart 16
4. Menelaus 19

Arranger's note

Of course, 'last pieces' are hardly conceived as such—rare is the composer who writes a final work and lays down their pen knowing they will not pick it up again. Ralph Vaughan Williams's *Four Last Songs* may be 'last', but it is likely they were not even thought of by him as a set: 'Menelaus' and 'Procris' were to be part of one cycle, and 'Hands, Eyes, and Heart' and 'Tired' as part of another.

That said, as a sequence the four songs offer a beautiful snapshot of two aspects of Vaughan Williams's writing. Vaughan Williams wrote for amateur choirs all his life. Like his younger colleague Britten he was able to write accessible music for the inexperienced singer that wears its learning lightly while losing none of its emotion. The middle two songs, 'Tired' and 'Hands, Eyes, and Heart', are simple and affecting, and in arranging them for unaccompanied choir I have tried to retain their simplicity.

'Procris' and 'Menelaus' show a different side to Vaughan Williams's writing. This is the Vaughan Williams of mystery and intense colour, of swirling mists and (occasionally dark) magic. The ever-shifting harmonies in these pieces offer both a challenge and an opportunity to the arranger. I have tried to harness some of the floating magic of Prospero in 'The Cloud-Capp'd Towers', and aimed to splash an extra dab of colour to Vaughan Williams's already fantastical piano score.

All four pieces would benefit from a nimble and flexible approach to choral singing. The pieces want, I think, to sound as artless and as effortless as possible—at times as if they were blowing about on the breeze—while at the same time the accompanying vocal lines in particular need to move exactly together, the singers always aware of what is happening in the other parts.

This arrangement was commissioned by the London Festival of Contemporary Church Music and first performed in 2022 to celebrate the 150th anniversary of the birth of Ralph Vaughan Williams.

Duration: *c.*10 minutes

This arrangement was commissioned by the London Festival of Contemporary Church Music and first performed in 2022 to celebrate the 150th anniversary of the birth of Ralph Vaughan Williams

Four Last Songs

Ursula Vaughan Williams

RALPH VAUGHAN WILLIAMS
arr. Jonathan Wikeley

1. Procris

(1958)

Music by Ralph Vaughan Williams, poems by Ursula Vaughan Williams © Oxford University Press 1960.
This arrangement © Oxford University Press 2023. All rights reserved.

Printed in Great Britain

OXFORD UNIVERSITY PRESS, MUSIC DEPARTMENT, GREAT CLARENDON STREET, OXFORD OX2 6DP
The Moral Rights of the Composer, Author, and Arranger have been asserted. Photocopying this copyright material is ILLEGAL.

9
the yel - low flowers show spring, the grass is green,
mm
mm
mm
mm
mm
12
be - fore a gen - - - tle
p stagger breathing
mm
p stagger breathing
mm
p stagger breathing
mm

15
wind the thin trees lean towards the rush - es, the
18
rush - es to the tide.
pp
She
pp murmured
Will not see, will not see,
pp murmured
Will not see, will not see,
pp murmured
Will not see, will not see,
pp

22
will not see the green spring turn to sum - mer,
will not see, will not see, will not see, turn to sum - mer,
will not see, will not see, will not see, turn to sum - mer,
will not see, will not see, will not see, turn to sum - mer,
25
sum - mer go in a long gold - en dusk towards the
sum - mer go in a long gold - en dusk towards the
sum - mer go in a long gold - en dusk towards the
sum - mer go in a long gold - en dusk towards the

28
snow, with eyes so lit by love that ev - 'ry - thing
snow, with eyes so lit by love that ev - 'ry - thing
snow, with eyes so lit by love that ev - 'ry - thing
snow, with eyes so lit by love that ev - 'ry - thing
31
burned, flowed, grew, blos - somed, moved on
burned, flowed, grew, blos - somed, moved on
burned, flowed, grew, blos - somed, moved on
burned, flowed, grew, blos - somed, moved on

33
ppp
foot or wing with the guessed rhythm of e - ter - ni - ty.
foot or wing with the guessed...
foot or wing with the guessed...
foot or wing with the guessed...
36
mp
All her hope and will flowed from her un - a -
p stagger breathing
uh
(p)

40
-vail - - ing and she knew dark - ness, as her eyes know now
43
pp
shut to the day-light, and des - pair pre - vail - ing she saw no
mm
saw
pp
saw no
mm
mm
(pp)

47
way to go.
way...
way to...
way to...
way...
mm
pp

2. Tired

(1956)

*taken from a mixture of sopranos and altos, always with a mind to the overall balance.

*taken from a mixture of tenors and basses, always with a mind to the overall balance.

16
-pair or hope di - vide me from your side.
-pair or hope di - vide me from your side.
uh
uh
uh
uh

19
Tempo primo
pp
I shall re - mem - ber fire - light on your sleep - ing
pp
I shall re - mem - ber fire - light on your sleep - ing
mm
pp
mm
mm
mm
pp

22
face, I shall re - mem-ber sha - dows grow-ing
face, I shall re - mem-ber sha - dows grow-ing
(S2 to the fore)
mm
mm
25
Ad lib.
deep - er as the fire fell to ash - es and the
deep - er as the fire fell to ash - es.
27
a tempo
min - - utes passed.
mm
mm
mm

3. Hands, Eyes, and Heart

(?1956)

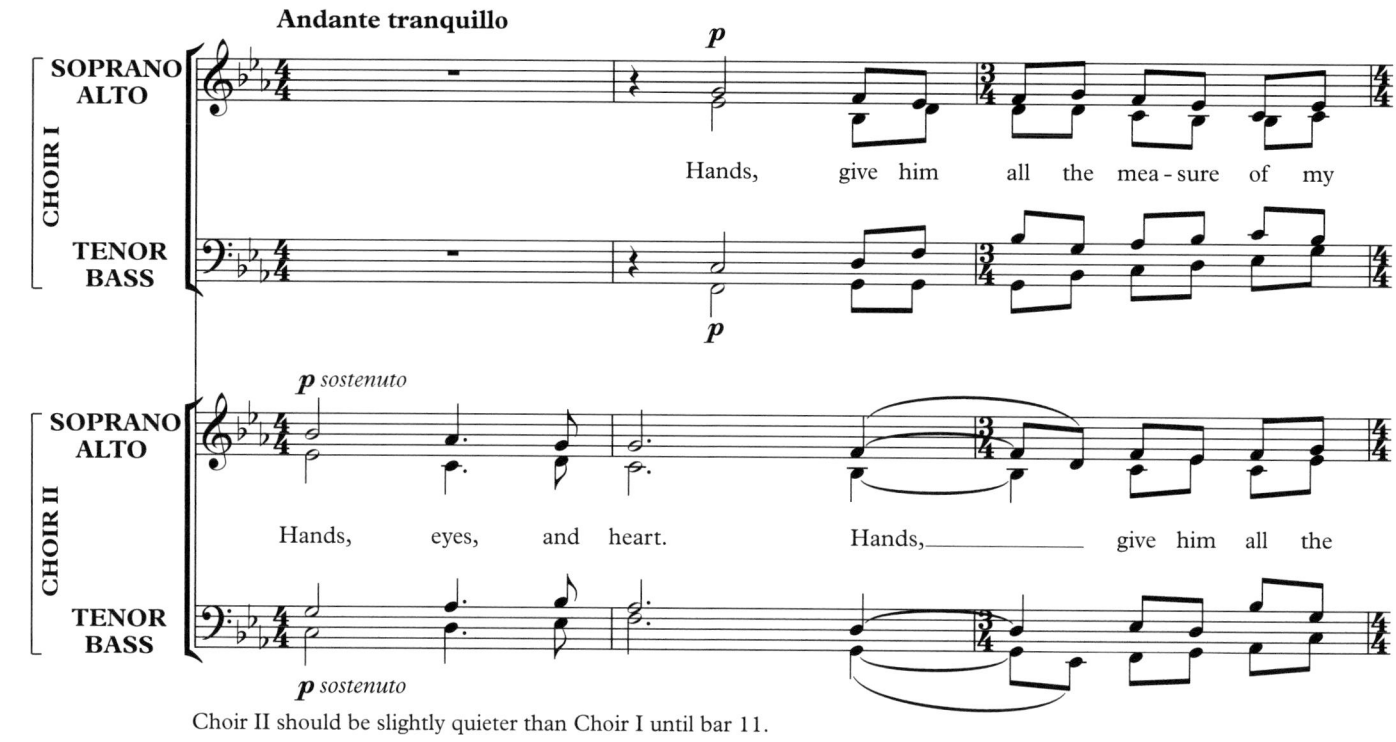

Choir II should be slightly quieter than Choir I until bar 11.

7
deep pools of truth,
deep pools of truth, where he may see a thought more
deep pools of truth, see,
deep pools of truth,
deep pools of truth, where he may
word. Eyes, be
deep pools of truth,
deep, truth,
10
mf
whole than con - stan - cy. Heart, in his
con - stan - cy.
mf
mf
see a whole mark of con - stan - cy. Heart, in his
mf

13
p
keep - ing, be at rest and live as mu - sic and
keep - ing be at rest,
p
p
keep - ing, be at rest, his keep - ing be at rest, and
p
keep - ing be at rest, rest, and
p

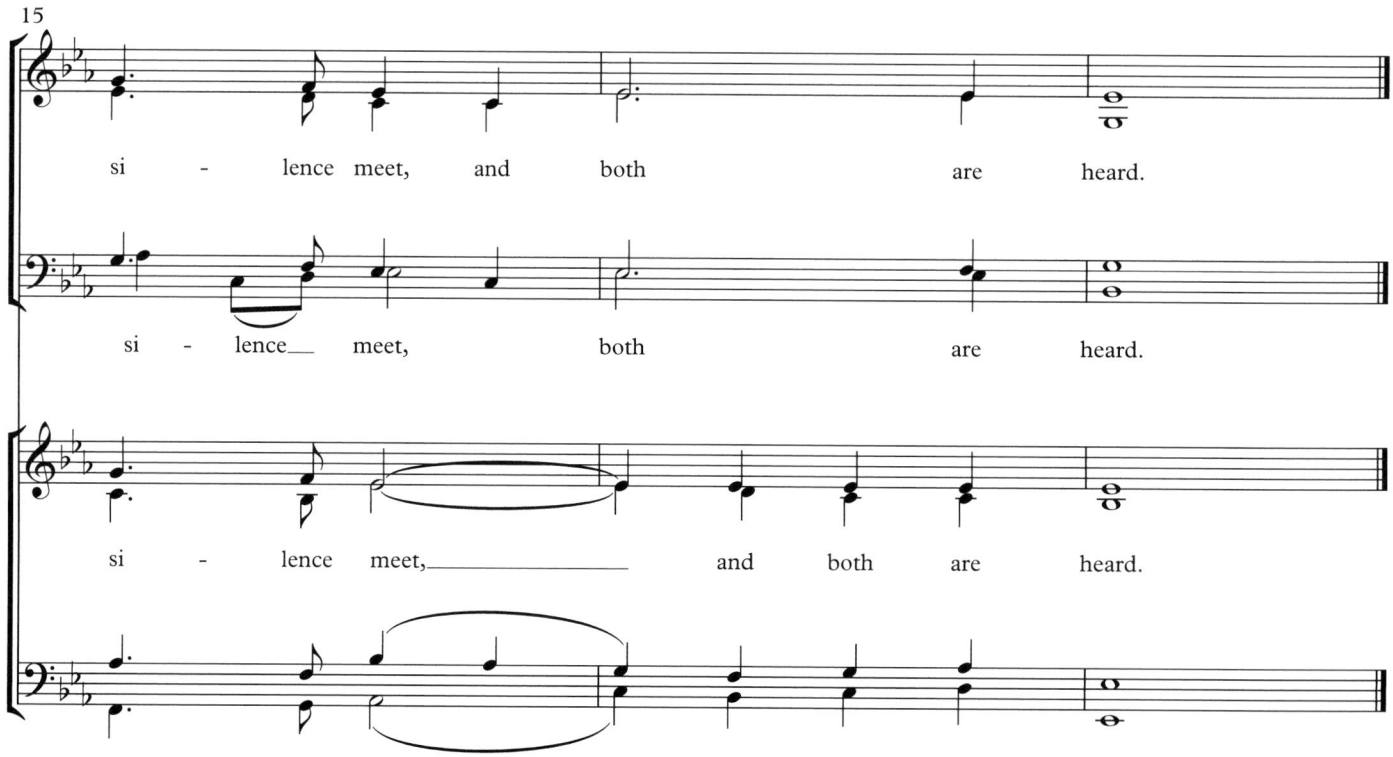
15
si - lence meet, and both are heard.
si - lence meet, both are heard.
si - lence meet, and both are heard.

4. Menelaus

(1954)

8
mp
thought re - mem - bers, go - ing from rose to rose a -
mp
that your thought re - mem - bers, go - ing from rose to
mp
13
- long the ter - rac - es and stay - ing to gaze at the
rose a - long the ter - rac - es and stay - ing to
18
mf
p
vines and reeds and i - ris be - side the
mf
gaze at the vines and reeds and i - ris be -
mf
p

22
pp
lake in the morn - ing haze.
p
pp
-side the lake in the morn - ing haze.
pp
26
sea - winds
For - get - ting the place you are in where the cold sea - winds
30
go cry - ing like gulls on the beach where the horned sea pop - pies
pp

33
(pp)
grow.
Home - sick
36
wan - der - er, you will come home
T.B. whisper 'will you come home?', each singer at a different speed.
39
to a home more
(pp)
to a home, a home more
(pp)

41
an - cient, wait - ing your re - turn:
an - cient, wait - ing your re - turn:
44
sea frets the steps that lie
pp una corda
46
green un - - - - der waves

48
and swal - lows nest be - low
50
lin - - tel and eaves:
52
mp
there lamps are kin - dled for you, they will burn till you
mp
mp tre corde

55
come, how - ev - er late you come,
come, you come, how - ev - er late you come,
come, how - ev - er late you come,
3
pp
58
p
till the west wind's shel - ter - ing
p
61
wing folds round your sail and

64
brings you to
brings you to land.
Stretch out your
brings you to
f
f
f
67
hand,
ff
69
pp
mur - mur - ing, lap - ping sea and the
and the
pp
pp

72
lamps and the wel - come wait to draw you home to
lamps wel - come wait, draw you home, you home to
75
rest. You shall come home and love
rest.
pp

79
and lay your heart on her
shall fold you in joy
and lay your heart on her...
8va

83
breast.
pp
mm
mm
mm
pp
mm
mm
pp